Dive Into

ACTION!

Find Your Niche In
Times of Uncertainty

Gary Lim, M.A.

DORATO PRESS

Dedicated to my wife Judy, who travels with me on

the Road to Gumption and anywhere else I might write about,

and to our daughter, who keeps asking me when my next book will be done,

no matter what it might be about.

DIVE INTO ACTION! FIND YOUR NICHE IN TIMES OF UNCERTAINTY. Copyright © 2009 by Gary Lim. All rights reserved. Printed and bound in the United States of America. No part of this book may be used or reproduced in any manner whatsoever without written permission except in the case of brief quotations embodied in critical articles and reviews. For information address Dorato Press, P. O. Box 71, Manlius, NY 13104.

FIRST EDITION

Publisher's Cataloging-in-Publication Data

Lim, Gary.

Dive into ACTION! : find your niche in times of uncertainty / Gary Lim.: -- 1st ed.

p. ; cm.

ISBN: 978-0-578-01823-2

1. Career development. 2. Job hunting United States. 3. Employees Dismissal of. 4. Unemployed--Psychology. I. Title.

HF5381 .L563 2009

650.14   2009903205

For further information:
315-885-1532
www.ActionPronto.com
www.BooksByGaryLim.com

Also by Gary Lim

Let It Fly!
Defy the Laws of Business Gravity and
Keep Your Company Soaring

The Road to Gumption:
Using Your Inner Courage To Balance
Your Work and Personal Life

"Our greatest glory is not in never falling,
but in rising every time we fall."

— Confucius

Introduction

Whether the economy is considered "bad", or is "good", we will inevitably experience times of uncertainty. When the economic situation is challenging, job losses and company downsizings become one of the largest sources of uncertainty, not only for those who lose their jobs, but also for those who remain. Even as the economy becomes friendlier, however, times of uncertainty can still affect us as companies and organizations adjust to conditions of growth.

No matter what the cause of your uncertainty, whether you are employed or not, my mantra still remains:

"Uncertain times call for certain action."

In times of uncertainty, you need to take action. If you are a victim of a job loss, the action centers on what you need to do to find the next step in your career, whether it is another job, another industry, or even self-employment. If you are still in a job, but feel or know that your situation will be changing soon, the same need for action applies to you as well.

To focus on this need for action, I turned the word "action" into an acronym that serves as an iterative cycle – a reminder – of proceeding with your action plan:

A is for **Accept**

C is for **Connect**

T is for **Transform**

I is for **Implement**

O is for **Objective**

N is for **Nerves**

When you remember the word ACTION, you do the things each letter represents, which helps you stay working toward your goals. You don't let yourself fall into the trap of "I'll wait and see what develops", where that leaves your outcome truly to chance and luck.

Many people think others have all the luck. But most of the people who seem to be lucky, actually work hard to create their luck. They take action, and they stick to it.

In this story, the fictional character of Bill McNolten is a man who has been at one company for the past 15 years. He suddenly finds himself without a job, a victim of a layoff. This is a wrenchingly new experience for him, a major upheaval that is at first an emotional roller coaster.

As he works his way through the initial feeling of crisis with the support of both his wife and college-age daughter, Bill gradually begins to learn and discover on his own what he needs to do to get to his next goal. And that is to take ACTION, as I have previously described in its acronym form of the word.

I know the feelings well. To lose a job unexpectedly, and then to have to look for a new one, is tremendously stressful. To be forced to look for a new job, even while still in the current one, can be just as stressful. I have experienced both situations in my past career history, during my own times of uncertainty.

You must keep the faith as you act. As Winston Churchill once said, "The pessimist sees difficulty in every opportunity. The optimist sees opportunity in every difficulty."

With this quick-reading story of Bill McNolten, I hope you benefit from the lessons of ACTION, and draw strength from them. So as you embark on your journey, remember to always Dive into ACTION, and work toward your goals!

Gary Lim
info@ActionPronto.com

Contents

Prologue – The News

The door swung open and banged against the door stop, bouncing back toward the man walking through. He raised his forearm to block the impact, sending the door back along its arc. Ricocheting once more off the door stop, the door swung shut with a loud slam.

Bill McNolten almost threw his briefcase onto the kitchen table and looked at the clock on the wall. 10:25 in the morning. It felt strange to be home from work at 10:25 in the morning on a weekday. But here he was. And no one else was home.

Almost 15 years, he thought. I've been with that company almost 15 years, and this is the thanks I get. To be home at 10:25 on a weekday. His mind replayed the conversation that occurred that morning, soon after he had arrived at his office.

"Hey Bill, got a minute?" his boss poked his head in Bill's office. "Can you come down to my office?"

"Sure, Mark," said Bill, as he grabbed a notepad and followed him two doors down the hallway. The men entered the office, and Mark closed the door.

"Have a seat." With his palm outstretched, Mark indicated the small round conference table in one corner of his office. Both men seated themselves.

Bill opened his notepad to the next empty page and looked at Mark. "So, what's on your mind?"

"Actually, a lot," admitted Mark. He seemed distracted. "It's been a lousy couple of months."

"I can imagine, with the downsizing we've been going through." Bill nodded sympathetically. He had been reporting to Mark for about three years, but the two men had known each other from when Mark first joined the company ten years ago.

Mark eyes seemed to be fixed on a spot on the edge of the table. "Yeah." He sighed.

Still looking at the spot on the table, Mark continued, "And it just got worse. Because now I have to tell one of my good friends and colleagues that we have to part company." He looked up and met Bill's gaze.

Bill looked at him, reading his expression, and blinked twice. A long silent moment ensued.

"You mean ... ?" Bill trailed off.

Mark nodded his head and sighed again. "I'm afraid so, Bill."

Bill stared at Mark, but for a moment saw only what seemed to be white noise. When the image cleared, Mark was still looking at him with an expression that was somehow simultaneously uncomfortable and forlorn.

"You're laying ... *me* off?" Bill asked in disbelief, gesturing toward himself.

Mark could only nod his head again. "I don't know what to say, Bill."

"Well, how about telling me why?" Bill's shock started its transformation into anger.

Mark shifted uncomfortably in his seat. "You know how the higher-ups are looking at the product lines and combining some of the organizations. Your line is one of those." He looked at Bill almost pleadingly. "I tried to argue the case for keeping your line separate, but they decided otherwise."

"Well, I guess your argument wasn't good enough." Bill looked away for the first time since the news broke, and stared at the ceiling. He snapped his head back down, eyes flashing angrily at Mark. "I wish you would have asked me to help build your case for you!"

And maybe it wouldn't have made any difference at all, Bill thought glumly as he sat down at his kitchen table, jacket still on. The rest of his meeting with Mark was like being in a haze, with Mark outlining the severance package he had negotiated hard to earn for Bill. And the visit with human resources to sign out, that was like being in the Twilight Zone, with terms like "COBRA" and "outplacement" just floating by in space.

Bill couldn't even spend much time saying goodbye to his co-workers. Strangely enough, not many of them were around. He just collected his personal items from his office, of course leaving the company-issued laptop and cell phone, and went out to his car. Which he had parked only about 90 minutes before, when he first arrived at the office.

Driving out of the parking lot, Bill wasn't really sure where to go, so he just headed home. He was numb. He didn't even think about calling his wife Carolyn at her office, not because he didn't want to, but simply because he didn't think of it. He was too numb.

So here he was, sitting at his kitchen table, at now 10:33 in the morning on a weekday. Not only was he home for the day, he was home, period. What now?

Taking a deep breath, he pulled out his personal cell phone and hit the speed dial for his wife's number.

Chapter 1 – It Sinks In

"They did what?!" Carolyn was tilted back in her chair when Bill called. She abruptly sat forward, the chair's recoil almost throwing her onto her desk. "How could they do that? You've been there almost 15 years!"

"I know," said Bill, elbows on the kitchen table at home. "It stinks. But Mark did say that he tried fighting for my line. And I think he's being honest with me. The senior executives see it another way."

"Obviously not the right way." Carolyn slapped the top of her desk, then sighed. "I'm sorry, honey. What can I do? Do you want me to take the rest of the day off?"

"No, I'm okay," Bill replied. "We can talk more tonight. I'm just going to get my head together first."

"You sure? I can tell my boss something came up."

"No, really honey, I'm good." Bill was actually feeling slightly better after breaking the news to his wife. "Just work your day, and don't think much about it. Remember, we've got some severance coming, so there's no need to panic."

The couple bid their goodbyes and Bill ended the call. He sat there for a moment, drumming his fingers on the tabletop, thinking about his next move, when his cell phone rang.

Looking at the caller ID screen, Bill's face lit up in spite of the events of the morning. A call from his daughter Rachel always brought a smile to his face. He flipped open the phone.

"How's my little girl doing?"

"C'mon Dad, you know I'm not so little anymore," said Rachel with a laugh. This was the familiar start of their greeting.

"Well, you know what I say … you'll always be my little girl, even when you're all grown up!" They both laughed together. Rachel was a senior at Rosenbluth College, about a three-hour drive from home.

"So what's up?" Bill asked his daughter.

"Dad, I need some help. It's time for on-campus recruiting to get underway full swing, and there's not much happening. Career Services says that most companies are under a hiring freeze right now, or are being even more selective than they've been before."

Bill stood up and crossed the family room to the door that opened onto their back deck, looked out and continued to listen.

Rachel went on, "Even though some of the companies have let some people go, they're still hiring from colleges for entry-level positions. But it's pretty competitive."

"That's for sure," agreed her father.

"I think I'll need your help in trying to figure out how to get some of those companies to notice me, Dad."

Bill stood silent, thinking for a moment.

"Dad? Are you there?"

"Oh, sorry Rache. I was just thinking. Of course I'll help you with your search. Actually, it's something we can end up doing together, because I'm in the same boat. I just got laid off this morning."

"*What?* " Rachel was startled, to say the least.

Bill told his daughter what had happened at his company earlier.

"Are we going to be okay, Dad? I mean, with my finishing school and everything?" asked Rachel, concern at the edges of her voice.

"No worries, honey. Your school is paid for with money we put away years ago. Besides, when you're this close to graduating, your mom and I would absolutely want you to finish." Bill turned and walked back to the kitchen table. "You've worked too hard for this."

"What are you going to do now?"

Bill held the phone between his shoulder and his ear as he took off his jacket. "Well, I'm going to start dusting off the resume and getting it updated. I probably should have been doing that all along, but never got to it, I guess."

"Well Dad, now's your chance."

"Right. The company is also giving me a few months' access to outplacement services, to help me with some of the details of looking for the next position. Sometimes those things are also good as kind of a support group, too."

Bill drummed his fingers on the kitchen table and continued. "A support group might be good. I hear it's lonely work, looking for a job. I don't know. I haven't had to do it in awhile."

His daughter's voice reached out from the phone, comfort to his ears. "I'll be your support group, Dad!" She laughed.

"Thanks, my girl." Bill brightened and smiled into the phone. "Like I said, maybe we can work on this together as a team. We both need to find jobs now, don't we?"

"Sure do. Where do we start?" Even though Rachel was only 21, Bill found her amazingly even-keel beyond her years. She could take things in stride, then move on.

"Let me get my act together in the next couple of days, then I'll call you again."

"Do you want me to send you a copy of my resume, Dad?"

Bill stood up and again walked over to the deck door to gaze out at the trees that bordered their backyard. "No, we've got to get our mindset straight first," he said thoughtfully.

"Mindset? What do you mean?"

His eyes snapped into focus again as clarity hit him. "We've got to figure out what we're going for, before we go for it. It won't do us any good to have a resume for a job that we might not be interested in, right?"

Rachel was puzzled. "But I thought the resume is the same one you use for any job."

"It is and it isn't," answered Bill. "The information stays the same, like where you worked and what positions you had, but some of the other things might be put differently, depending on what you want to do."

He was starting to see a path, starting to come out of the fog that first enshrouded him when Mark told him he was being let go. Despite the shock of the morning's developments, Bill started to feel some energy creep back into his voice.

"This morning caught me so much by surprise that I'm forgetting the things I learned when I was on the other side of the fence." Bill sat down on a nearby couch in the family room. "Now it's time for me to pay attention to that again."

"You lost me, Dad." Rachel was just a bit exasperated. "First we're talking resumes, then mindset, and now the other side of the fence. What fence?"

Bill laughed. It seemed strange to laugh on a day like this, but it felt good. Talking to both Carolyn and Rachel was helping to ease the burden.

"I meant, when I was the one doing the hiring. There were things I looked for in candidates, and what I need to do now is to remember those things to shape how we present ourselves, now that we're the candidates."

"If you say so."

"I say so." Bill grinned. "Anyway, let me get my head together and we'll talk again."

"Okay, Dad. I have to get to class soon anyhow. Say hi to Mom!"

Father and daughter said their goodbyes, and Bill flipped his phone closed. He sat for a moment, tapping his phone on the side of his jaw. Kids always keep you grounded, he mused. Rachel had taken the news of his layoff in stride, showed her concern, asked a question, then moved right along. And that's what he needed to do, too.

Bill got up and headed to the fridge for something to drink.

Chapter 2 – Up and Down

Bill's cell phone rang as he finished taking a drink from the bottle of water he fetched from the refrigerator. He picked up the phone and pushed Talk.

"Hello, this is Bill."

"Hey Bill, how are you doing? I just heard the news." Jim was another product line director whose office was a couple of doors down from Bill's.

"Well, okay I suppose, all things considered," replied Bill. He took another drink from his water bottle. "A little shellshocked, though."

Jim was sympathetic. "I can imagine. Well, maybe I can't. You had no idea?"

"Absolutely none. Did you hear any rumors?" Bill was close enough to Jim to be able to ask the question and know that Jim would answer it truthfully.

"Nothing. We just went through the cycle as you know, where we had to lay out the plans for the coming quarters. I presume you did the same thing. But after that, we didn't hear anything from management, not even a follow-up question."

"Me neither." Bill was back in the family room, plunked down on the couch. "Maybe that should have been a sign for me, no follow-up questions. They already made up their minds."

"I don't think you can second-guess it, Bill. Like I said, we heard nothing either, and now that you're gone, some of us are getting a little nervous around here." Jim had closed the door to his office by then. "We didn't think it would ever happen to you!" He let out a short nervous laugh.

"Yeah, well that makes two of us," agreed Bill gloomily.

"So I know it's only been an hour or two, but what are you going to do now?"

"I don't know, the usual I guess. Find my resume and polish it up. Go see what the outplacement thing is all about." Bill was starting to feel down again about the morning's sudden developments.

A flash of anger shot through him as he gestured wildly. "Dammit Jim, you would think that they would have been more sensitive about things!" Bill's hand struck the bottle of water and sent it flying onto the floor. Good thing he had capped it.

"What do you mean, more sensitive?" asked Jim gently.

"Well, I've been with the company for 15 years! And I've had my share of giving my soul to them over the years. The long hours, weekends. You'd think that they would offer me another position instead of casting me off." The mood swings of being laid off were now starting to show.

Jim wanted to be soothing. "What kind of job could they have offered you, Bill? You're a special guy in what you do. There's not anything else that you would want to do in the company, right?"

"*I don't know!* " Bill exploded. "What are you asking me for? I wasn't even given the choice!" He slumped down in his seat.

There was an awkward pause. Jim figured he'd better move along. "Well, let me know if there's anything I can do. And stay in touch, okay?"

"Okay," replied Bill. His anger had melted into dejection. "Oh, and thanks for calling, Jim." He tried to make it sound like he meant it.

"No problem. Take care of yourself."

Bill flipped his phone closed and put it back in his pocket. He got up and retrieved the fallen bottle of water, unscrewed the top and took a large swig.

This is exhausting, he thought. I just feel like taking a nap. His phone rang again. Bill fished it out of his pocket and saw it was Carolyn calling.

"Hi there," he said with forced normalcy.

"How are you doing, honey?" His wife's voice had a layer of concern on it.

"I don't know, doing okay I guess. A little up and down, though," admitted Bill. "I think I just yelled at Jim, and didn't mean to." He recounted the conversation the two men had just had.

"Are you sure you don't want me to come home?" Carolyn asked.

"No, really, you don't have to," answered Bill.

"Well, how about meeting me for lunch, then?" Carolyn's office was only about 20 minutes from the house.

Bill brightened at the thought of it. They rarely got to eat lunch together during the week. "That might be a good idea." He would pick her up at noon.

What was left of the morning went by for Bill in a bit of a blur. He wandered around the house, almost looking for something to do. Getting on the home computer, he considered sending out some email to bring some of his contacts up to date, but hesitated. In the middle of composing the first email, he stopped and canceled the message without finishing it.

When it was time to leave for his wife's office, Bill jumped into his car and started it up. As the garage door closed and he backed down the driveway, he noticed how odd it felt to be doing this in the middle of a weekday.

"Other than Jim, have you heard from anyone else?" Carolyn took a bite out of the roll she had buttered. They were now seated in a restaurant not far from her office.

"No, he's the only one so far." Bill was in a gloomy mood again as he stirred the ice in his Coke endlessly. "And I don't think I was very nice to him at the end."

"Well, I'm sure he understood."

Bill looked up, suddenly remembering. "Come to think of it, I did hear from someone else – Rachel."

"Oh?" Carolyn broke into a smile. "How is she? And how did she know about what happened to you this morning?"

Leaning forward, Bill put his elbows on the table. "She didn't. She just happened to call to ask about something else. That's what's so ironic."

Their lunch entrees arrived as the server put their plates down in front of them. When all was set and the server retreated, Carolyn asked, "What was so ironic?"

"Rache was calling me to ask for some advice about finding a job," answered Bill with a mouthful of sandwich. "Isn't that something! Like I'm going to be chock full of advice right now!"

Seeing her husband's changing mood, Carolyn put her fork down and gazed steadily into his eyes. "But you do have a lot of experience, dear, and you know that would be a great help to our daughter," she said gently.

Bill looked at her, then looked away as his eyes teared up. He blinked rapidly and took a couple of breaths.

"I don't know, Carolyn. I haven't had to do this in 15 years. I'm so used to being on the hiring side of the fence!" His voice sounded almost anguished.

"But that's what I mean," she continued. "You know what it's like from the hiring side. So you know what people are looking for. That's your advantage." She reached out across the table and put her hand over her husband's.

Bill had recovered from the emotion of the moment, and picked up his sandwich again. He took a bite as Carolyn continued.

"You and Rachel are both looking now. Maybe you could work with her and give her some guidance, too." She picked up her fork to resume eating.

"You know, that's actually what I told Rachel." Bill took a gulp from his Coke. He smiled at the memory of the conversation. "She said she'd be my support group!"

Carolyn nodded as she worked on her salad. "That's our girl!"

Parts of his conversation with his daughter started to return to Bill. He put his sandwich down.

"I just remembered, I was saying to Rachel that I needed to focus on the things that I looked for in candidates when I was doing the hiring." Bill waved a French fry in the direction of his wife. "Just like you said a moment ago."

Carolyn nodded, picking another roll while he continued.

"And because I knew what to look for then, as a guy looking for a job now, I need to be sure that I present those things to people I interview with." Bill ate the French fry he was using as a pointer.

He swallowed and sat back, wiping his mouth with his napkin. Silent for a moment, he sighed.

"I've got to tell you, it's scary though. I haven't been in this situation for a long time. It's been people approaching me for jobs, not the other way around."

Bill looked over at his wife, uncertainty written all over his face.

"I know," replied Carolyn sympathetically. "But it will work out. You know the things that you need to do, and you know that you can do them. So all you have to do, is do them!"

"That's way easier said than done." Bill went back to eating his lunch.

They were silent for a few minutes, just concentrating on their food and their thoughts. Carolyn put her fork down and leaned back in her chair.

"At least, for now, we can count on my job, knock on wood." She made a gesture of knocking on the table. "So I think you ought to take this opportunity to really think about what it is you'd like to do next."

Bill slurped the last of his Coke through his straw. "What do you mean?"

"I mean figure out what it is that you like. I never said anything to you, but in the last year or two, you seemed to be less excited about your job than you used to be." Carolyn leaned forward for emphasis.

Bill sat back and gazed at the ceiling for a moment. He met his wife's eyes again. "I think some of that had to do with the cutbacks that were going on."

Carolyn shook her head. "No, I mean even before that, you seemed to be less passionate about your job than before."

He didn't answer at first. "Well, I have to admit, I did have some thoughts about whether what I was doing was starting to get old. But each time I reminded myself about our financial plan and Rachel's college fund."

"That's what I mean about this opportunity." Carolyn locked eyes with her husband. "We already took care of Rachel's college needs. Maybe it's time to look at your needs."

"I just assumed that I would start applying for the types of jobs that I've been doing all these years." Bill sounded uncertain.

"I think you should still do that." His wife nodded. "But I also think you should at least look into other things you might be interested in."

"Like what?"

Carolyn drummed her fingers on the tabletop as she thought. "Well, you mentioned wanting to start your own business someday. And also about working in a completely different type of company, something not related to technology or manufacturing."

Bill remembered and smiled wryly. "I think I said those things during a time when I was a little fed up with some of the politics that were going on." He took a sip of water and continued.

"Of course, being a little fed up then is nothing like what I feel now."

His wife gave him a sympathetic look. "I still think that it's worth it for you to consider those things now, if only just to think them through and eliminate them."

"You're right." Bill looked up as the server came to deliver the check. He reached for his wallet.

"Why don't you let me get that, dear," said Carolyn. "I don't often get a chance to take my husband to lunch!"

"Well … okay." Bill grinned.

After leaving the restaurant, they got into Bill's car and he drove back to Carolyn's office. As she got out she said, "I'll see you tonight. Do you need me to pick up anything on the way home?"

"Nope." Bill gave another wry grin and said sarcastically, "If I do, I've got plenty of time this afternoon to get it. I don't have any meetings planned!"

As Bill drove back home, he realized how much of the day had been up and down, quite an emotional ride.

Chapter 3 – Accept

B ack at the house, Bill walked in from the garage, tossed his jacket carelessly onto the couch and headed up the stairs. Might as well just change my clothes, he thought.

As he finished changing into a pair of jeans, his cell phone rang.

"Hello?"

"Bill, it's Marty." It was one of their neighbors a couple of doors down, a retired former company owner. "I saw you drive up. Are you available to help me move a shelf in my house?"

"Sure. I'll be right over." Bill went downstairs and out the front door.

As he walked up the street and approached the house, Marty walked out of the garage smiling.

"Taking the day off? You picked a good one!"

Bill felt a little twinge in his stomach. "Uh, yeah, I guess I did." He smiled weakly. "Anyhow, what can I help you with?"

Marty needed an extra pair of hands to help him get a freestanding bookcase from one room to another, without scratching the floor. It took the men all of three minutes to get the task done. They walked out through Marty's garage.

"Well, thanks again Bill," said Marty extending his hand. "That was a big help."

Bill returned the handshake. "No problem. Glad to help anytime."

"So what are you up to the rest of today?"

"Uh … I don't know, probably just get some house projects done that I've been meaning to get to." Bill was uncomfortable. The two men chatted a few minutes longer before they parted.

As Bill walked back to his house, he thought about what had just happened. For some reason he had a hard time telling Marty about the developments from the morning. Bill was not sure why he didn't tell him, and because he didn't say anything he was now conflicted about it.

Why didn't I say anything, he thought. It's not like Marty would think any differently about me. Or would he?

Bill returned to his house and let himself in, still bothered by his reluctance to tell Marty about his new job situation. Perhaps it's pride, he thought a little guiltily, never being one to admit that pride or vanity would drive him to act in any particular way.

Besides, he reasoned to himself, he might be able to land something fairly quickly, so he wouldn't need to tell anyone who didn't really need to know.

Bill's thoughts were interrupted by his cell phone ringing again. Without looking at the display, he answered.

"Hello, this is Bill."

"Hi Dad!"

"How's my little girl doing?" He smiled as he said the familiar opening line.

"Pretty good. Just got out of class. Actually, I was calling to see how you were doing."

"Oh, okay, I guess. I had lunch with your mother today."

In her dorm room 150 miles away, Rachel leaned back on her bed and crossed her legs under her. "But how are *you* doing, Dad?"

Bill thought for a moment. "Tell you the truth, Rache, it's been up and down all day. I can't say it's been the most exciting day I've ever had."

He paused. "Well, maybe it's been exciting in one way, but I'm not very excited about the way it's gone."

"Sorry, Dad."

"Hey by the way, Marty from up the street asked about you today." Marty had known Rachel since she was little.

"Oh? Were you telling him about what happened at work?"

Bill hesitated. "Uh, no I didn't. He called to ask me to help him move a bookcase in his house."

"And you didn't tell him about today?" Rachel leaned forward on her bed.

"No."

"Why not, Dad? Didn't you tell me that he stays in contact with a lot of people he knows from business?"

"That's right, he does."

"So why didn't you say anything to him?" Rachel could be annoyingly persistent sometimes. She had always been like that even as a child.

"Oh I don't know." Bill was a little exasperated at being questioned by his own daughter. "I didn't have the chance to bring it up, I guess. He did ask me if I was taking the day off, though."

Rachel kept it up. "That would have been the time to tell him, wouldn't it?"

"Well I didn't!" Bill was more than a little exasperated now, perhaps a little self-conscious too. "And I really don't know why. Maybe I figured that he didn't need to know, especially if I land the next position pretty quickly."

Then Rachel said what he had perhaps been unwilling to think about all day.

"But Dad, what if you don't? What if it takes awhile to find the next position?"

Bill was silent. His daughter could be such a pain sometimes. But she was right.

"I ... suppose that maybe I'm still in a little bit of denial mode." By now Bill was sitting in the family room again. He leaned back on the couch and continued.

"That's probably it, I hate to say. I'm sitting here thinking – or hoping – that something else will come along pretty quickly, and that I won't need to have anyone know I've been out of work."

"But Dad, what's wrong with being out of work? It happens all the time. You read it in the news. You're the one who always told me that 'stuff happens'." There was that pragmatic Rachel again.

"Rache, I've never had it happen to me," protested Bill. "I've always been the one who was doing the hiring, or who other companies wanted to hire. So this is a new feeling for me."

"Right, but you also always told me that I need to get beyond things. I think your favorite saying to pound into my head was 'It is what it is. Don't make it what it isn't.' Why doesn't that apply to you?"

That was like a whack on the side of the head. Bill really did say that to her at times as she grew up. He didn't necessarily agree that he "pounded" it into her head, but he did make the point more than a few times.

"Okay Rache, you win." Bill couldn't help but grin. His daughter was getting to be like her old man. "I probably am guilty of being in denial today. Nothing like hearing my own words coming back at me from my own daughter to set me straight."

"I told you this morning, Dad, I'll be your support group." Miles away in her dorm, Rachel did a silent double-pump to celebrate making her point. "Besides, you told me that you just needed to get back to the other side of the fence, remember? So get back!"

"You're right. I need to remember that. Your mother also said the same thing, too, about getting back into the right frame of mind so I can market myself again. I guess I got thrown for a loop because I never imagined myself being in this situation."

He sighed. "It's been quite a day, Rache. The hardest thing is to accept what's happened and move on."

"I know, Dad. That's certainly what you taught me." She looked at her watch. "Oops, gotta run. I have to meet Amy over at the library."

"Okay, thanks for calling, Rache!" They said their goodbyes and ended the call.

Bill sat for a moment, still on the couch. Then he smiled. Just like his daughter to throw his oft-repeated words back at him, but it came at a good time. He got up and walked over to the home office, where the computer was.

J ust after 6 o'clock Carolyn came walking through the door from the garage into the kitchen. She put her things down in the hallway, and heard keyboard clicks coming from the home office.

Walking around the corner and through the door, she found Bill in the midst of staring at the computer display screen.

"Hi dear. What are you looking at?"

Bill swiveled in the chair to face his wife. "I was starting to look into some of the things that I had been thinking about a couple of years ago. Just trying to get some early ideas of what's out there."

Carolyn studied her husband's face carefully. "And how are you, Bill? How was the afternoon?"

Bill grinned. "Interesting. I got a call from my action coach. She set my head straight, after all these things that have happened today."

"Action coach?" Carolyn was puzzled. "Who is that?"

"Why, our daughter, of course." Bill laughed. "You should have heard her. She started the call by asking me how I was doing. She ended it by repeating one of my mantras back to me, and asked me why I was acting like it didn't apply to me."

He went on to tell his wife about the conversation that he and Rachel had earlier, and about seeing Marty before that.

Carolyn smiled and shook her head. "That's Rachel all right, telling it like it is. She probably got a kick out of making the point with one of your sayings."

"I'm sure she did. But I really needed the reminder. I was down in the dumps, feeling sorry for myself, and there was that measure of not wanting to accept what had happened this morning. But it happened, and I need to accept it."

He stood up and leaned against the bookcase. "And I also have to remember what I told someone else a long time ago, when I had to lay him off."

"What was that?"

"The guy was good at what he did, but the product line that he was in charge of didn't make it to the market because of some issues in development. Upper management decided that they didn't want to try to be in that business anymore, and since he was a specialist in that particular field, we didn't have a place for him."

Bill walked into the family room, continuing the story as Carolyn followed him.

"I had the tough job of notifying him that we were laying him off. He was not happy, of course. He thought that somehow he must have made someone in senior management mad, and that this must be their revenge."

"Was he mad at you?" Carolyn sat down on the couch.

Bill sat next to her. "No, he wasn't. But he kept asking me to find out who it was who must have been mad at him, and advise him on how to make it right.

"I told him that as far as I knew, no one was 'mad' at him, and that they all appreciated his efforts to that point. He even had a pretty generous severance package given the short amount of time he was with us."

Bill pondered the ceiling for a moment. "Come to think of it, even more generous than mine in some ways." He looked at Carolyn and countered her expression with a grin. "Just kidding."

"Anyway, I kept going around and around with this guy, trying to reassure him that no one was mad. He seemed intent on making the situation into something it wasn't.

"I finally said to him, 'Look, it's not personal. It's just business. We wanted to get into a new field, we were lucky enough to bring you on board to try to make it happen, but it didn't happen through events out of your control. It's not you. It's just business.' "

"Did he seem to understand that?" Carol was engrossed by the story.

"I thought so," replied Bill, crossing his ankles. "After I repeated 'it's just business' he seemed to settle down a bit. I think he was just used to doing a good job, and being let go was like a personal insult, even if it was a layoff. He ended up landing on his feet just fine with another company."

He turned toward Carolyn. "And that is what I need to remember too. That it's not personal, it's just business. The company didn't act against me this morning, it made a business decision."

Bill stood up and offered his hand to his wife. "So will you remind me about that, any time I forget?"

Carolyn took his hand and pulled herself off the couch. "I will, under one condition."

"What's that?"

"That we find something to eat." Carolyn gestured in the direction of the kitchen. "C'mon, I'm hungry."

Takeaways – "A" is for "Accept"

This is the most difficult part of the cycle – to accept your situation and to try to move beyond the feeling that it might not be "fair." It might have been totally unfair. Fair or unfair, the situation is what it is. This is not to minimize what happened to you, or to let the others off the hook. This is so you can start to put it behind you and move on to your own action plan.

It is far better to spend your energy looking forward to your next great opportunity, than to spend it looking back on what's happened and rehashing whether or not it was fair. On this I speak from personal experience.

Accept your situation, accept the uncertainty, and then move on. Admittedly this is much easier said than done, but you must do it. You will have "relapses" of emotions as time goes on, and you will experience ups and downs, but those episodes will become further apart and lesser in intensity.

In most situations, it really is not personal – it's not you, it's just business. Sometimes stuff happens in business, but it's not directed at you. Just get ready to figure out and act on your own action plan for your next big thing.

It is what it is. Don't make it what it isn't.

Chapter 4 – Connect

Over the next week, Bill did his best with the process of adjusting to his "new normal". He wasn't exactly settled in yet, but he was able to accept what had happened and was starting to get to the mindset he had first mentioned to his wife and daughter.

The other important thing he needed to realize was that he now had a job. That job was to find a new position. Or, if not a job similar to what he was doing before, to seek the next career move that would enable him to earn a living.

During the past few days Bill had been talking to Carolyn off and on about possibly going to the outplacement service center that the company had referred him to. The subject came up again after dinner.

"I don't know if I'm going to use the service," said Bill. They were sitting at the kitchen table, the remnants of takeout still visible on their plates.

"Why not?"

"Well, I don't know how much good it will do. As we already talked about, I know what the hiring side is looking for, so what else can they help me with?" Bill took a fork and lightly tapped it on the placemat in front of him.

Carolyn ran her fingers through her hair. "Don't they give you feedback on your resume, and have other resources for you to look at openings?"

"They do review your resume and give you comments," admitted Bill. "But I already know what I need to include in my resume. I'm not a novice at this, you know." He threw the fork down on the placemat.

The irritation in Bill's voice did not go unnoticed by Carolyn. She reached out and put her hand gently on top of his.

"No, you're not. But as you said several times in the last week, this is a new situation for you."

Bill's shoulders slumped slightly. No one said this was going to be easy.

Carolyn searched her husband's face with her gaze. "Why not just go and see what it's all about? It doesn't cost you anything, right?"

"Right. The company is paying for six months' access to the service." Bill stood up to put his plate in the sink.

"Then why not just take a look? You don't have to agree with everything they suggest to you."

Bill turned from the sink and leaned his backside on the counter's edge. He folded his arms across his chest.

"I guess so. I'm just not sure what they can add. I know how to do a resume. As for job-searching resources, those are all Web-based these days, so I can look from our computer at home."

Carolyn studied her husband for a moment. "Are you a little apprehensive about going to the outplacement office?"

"No. I don't know. Well, maybe." Bill unfolded his arms and sat back down in his chair at the table. He looked at Carolyn and shrugged his shoulders.

"I … I just feel so …" He trailed off.

His wife just looked at him, waiting for him to finish. Bill tried again to put his feelings into words.

"… so embarrassed, I suppose," he finished.

"Why would you be embarrassed, dear?" Carolyn was surprised.

"That I lost my job, I guess. After 15 years." He looked at her with a slightly lost look. "That it was me, and not someone else."

"Ah, it's the pride thing again," said Carolyn with a smile. "Now what did you ask me to remind you about, at the end of the first day?"

"Oh yeah … it's not personal, it's just business."

"Right. So I'm reminding you now." But they both knew it was going to take time; that was only natural.

"Okay, okay."

Carolyn looked at Bill. "So is that the main reason you're hesitating? Because your pride is bothering you?"

Bill looked a little sheepish. "I suppose so."

"That's not surprising." His wife nodded understandingly. "But you've got nothing to lose by using the service. After all, the other clients there are also in the same situation as you."

"You're right."

"So you'll go?"

"Yes. I guess I'll swallow my pride and do it."

Carolyn looked into her husband's eyes and spoke gently. "I know things have been tough on your emotions. But this is not a matter of swallowing your pride, because it's not you, remember?"

Bill nodded, saying nothing. His wife continued.

"There are a lot of people in the same situation. Even Rachel knows that. You told me. So there's nothing to be self-conscious about."

She got up and put her plate in the sink, then turned.

"If nothing else, you have more opportunity to talk about what you're looking for. You never know who might be listening, right?"

Bill nodded and got up to face his wife.

"You're right. And it would be a good opportunity to hone my pitch about what I'm looking for."

Carolyn plugged in the coffee pot. "At least you'll know what questions you get, and what seems clear and not so clear when you tell them."

"Okay. Settled." Bill fetched a couple of coffee cups from the cabinet. "I'll call tomorrow and make an appointment to check it out."

He put the cups down on the counter and looked at his wife appreciatively.

"Thanks for all your support, honey. And for keeping me straight."

She smiled. "Sure. Somebody's got to do it. It might as well be your wife and daughter!"

B ill pulled into the sun-washed parking lot and found an empty space outside the three-story office building. He got out of his car holding the leather folder containing a writing pad and the draft of his resume tucked in the pocket.

Walking into the building, he found the elevator and punched the "2" button. When it reached the second floor, he paused for a moment, took a deep breath, then headed down the hall toward the suite.

Bill pushed the door open and approached the receptionist.

"Hi, I'm Bill McNolten."

The receptionist looked up with a smile and said, "Good morning. And what company were you with?"

He named his former employer as she consulted a list. Looking up again, she said, "Have a seat, and Shirley will be with you. Can I get you anything to drink?"

"No, thank you." Bill took a seat and looked around, surveying the landscape. Before long a well-dressed woman came around the corner.

"Hello, Bill? I'm Shirley. Come on in." He followed her into her office.

The next hour passed quickly, with Bill recounting his background and history. Shirley spent some time describing the process and the resources that Bill could access. Then she asked the question that Bill was half-expecting, but had not prepared for.

"So Bill, what are you looking to do next? More of the same? Or something different?"

Bill sat back in his chair to ponder the question. He answered carefully.

"To tell you the truth, I'm really not sure. My first reaction is to look for the same type of job that I've been doing for the past ten or more years. But my wife reminded me that this might be an opportunity to look into something different."

Shirley nodded in agreement. "And your wife is wise to remind you about that. There is that old saying 'when one door closes, another one opens'. I think you should at least go through the process of thinking about other things."

She leaned forward and rested her arms on her desk. "Not that you should change careers or industries, but it's just an opportunity to consider it."

"Oh, I agree with my wife. But at the moment I'm just not sure what else I would consider." Bill shrugged. "It's barely been two weeks since I got laid off."

Shirley nodded again and smiled. "Perfectly natural and expected. After 15 years at the same company, you certainly can't expect to figure out your next move in two weeks!"

The meeting concluded with her showing Bill where everything was located in the office, the coffee room, the computers, and other resources. After taking the copy of his resume for her later comment, Shirley told Bill he was welcome to stay and familiarize himself with things.

Well I'm here, so I might as well do some looking around, thought Bill as he sat down in front of an available computer. He started to delve into some Web sites that he knew listed current openings, and became engrossed for awhile.

"How are you? I'm Stan. Haven't seen you around."

Bill looked up and saw a man standing with his hand outstretched. He stood up and returned the handshake greeting.

"Bill McNolten. Pleased to meet you!" The men spent the next few minutes exchanging stories of their situations. Bill found it less awkward than he thought it would be, especially since Stan was in a similar situation, though the other man had been in job search mode for more than two months so far.

"I'm just getting started on this," apologized Bill, "but if you don't mind me asking, how are you going about your search? What are some of the things I ought to be thinking of doing?"

Stan thought for a moment. "If I had to emphasize one thing, I would say that you get out and connect with as many people as you can. Tell them that you're looking for a job, and what you're looking for. Don't be bashful. Now is not the time to be shy."

"Is that what you did?"

Stan nodded, and leaned his forearm on the top of a partition wall. "There are lots of Web sites where you can find suggestions and methods of connecting with people, including using social media.

"But the main thing is to get the word out. You need to find a job, and that requires the participation of other people."

Stan pulled out the empty chair next to Bill, and sat down. "I met a guy at a networking meeting a couple of weeks ago, that really illustrates this point. He had been laid off from his company. When I asked him how he was getting the word out, he answered, 'Oh, I haven't really told anyone yet. I'm waiting until I get the next position first.'"

Palms upraised, Stan continued, "So my question to him was, if you don't tell anyone, how do you expect to find a job?"

He dropped his hands and pointed at Bill. "Don't fall into that trap. There's no shame in looking for your next great opportunity. Nice meeting you!"

B ack at his house later that afternoon, Bill thought about Stan's words. It certainly made a lot of sense, and Bill was already feeling a little more comfortable about talking to others about his job search, even if he hadn't yet thought through all the options. After all, only two weeks had passed since he left the company.

The door from the garage opened, and Carolyn walked through, home from work. She put her things on the kitchen table and plunked down in one of the chairs.

"How was the meeting this morning?"

Bill proceeded to fill her in on the conversations that he had at the office.

"I seem to be getting more comfortable with talking about my situation," he concluded. "It's reassuring to hear that there are others in the same boat."

His wife nodded understandingly as Bill continued.

"I think I see my main mission in the coming days as having two parts – connect with as many people as I can, and at the same time, figure out what options I'd like to pursue."

Bill was starting to feel better about his direction going forward.

Takeaways – "C" is for "Connect"

The job now is to find a job, or at least the next destination in your career. This takes the involvement of others. You cannot be embarrassed or shy about this. There is no shame in looking for your next great opportunity.

And unless people know that you are looking, they cannot help you with your efforts.

Tell everyone you know that you are looking for your next opportunity. Ask them to keep their eyes and ears open, and to let you know if they hear of something that might seem interesting to you.

Get comfortable with discussing your new job – the job of finding your next opportunity, whether that is a new job, a new industry, or perhaps even self-employment.

If you're still employed but find yourself forced to look for a new position, there is some common sense discretion you will have to exercise. At least spread the word with people you trust who can be discreet on your behalf.

So don't be shy! As (English poet) Alfred Tennyson wrote, "The shell must break before the bird can fly."

Chapter 5 – Transform

The next couple of weeks found Bill entrenched more comfortably in his routine. Get up in the morning, exercise or go for a walk, have something to eat, then scan the top stories online and plan out his day.

He found that once he got over the emotions of being laid off, he could focus on the aspect of his job of finding a job. Well, he wasn't exactly over the emotions, but was starting to get beyond them. There admittedly were times when he would feel a twinge of anger over it all again. Those were the times when he reminded himself of what he had once told someone else, that it's not personal, it's just business. Then he would go back to doing what he needed to do.

Bill's latest focus was to look at what it is he might really like to do. At this point, he had already polished up his resume, taking some of the feedback given to him by Shirley at the outplacement office. His was angled more towards positions that were similar to the one he had left.

The more difficult thing to do was to think about what he might want to do that was different. During one of his visits to the office, he had a conversation with another job seeker, Dan.

"I'm thinking of going into my own business," said Dan.

"Any ideas of what that might be?"

"Not sure yet. There are a few ways to do this. Franchise model, independent rep, purchase a business, start from scratch." Dan scratched his head. "Each one has its pluses and minuses."

Bill leaned against a partition wall. "What are some of the pros and cons?"

"Well, if you're in a franchise, you have to first purchase one. Then depending on what business it is, you'd have to spend more money to set it up with equipment or whatever. After that you generally pay a percentage of sales to the franchise company for the length of your contract."

Dan gestured with his thumb pointing up. "Those bucks could go way up. But on the other hand, the franchise is supposed to bring you some brand recognition right away."

"What about the other ways?" Bill was not very familiar with the different forms of business.

"An independent rep probably won't cost you much upfront, but a lot of these business opportunities are structured like network marketing. That's where you recruit people under you to sell the products, and they recruit others, and so on." It looked like Dan had done his homework.

Bill asked, "You mean like a pyramid scheme?"

"No, these firms sell real products and are not pyramids, which are illegal. But I'm not sure network marketing is for me. I just have to give it some more thought."

Bill sat down in his chair again. "Then what about buying or starting a business?"

Dan shook his head. "That's the hard part. Both of those take upfront money also. And while I still have some of my severance cash, I'm a little nervous about taking most of it to launch a business."

He shrugged his shoulders. "It's a dilemma for me right now."

Bill thought for a moment. "Do you know what type of business you're interested in? I mean, what kinds of products or services?"

Dan took a sip from his coffee cup before answering. "Actually, not yet. I was just looking at the different forms and trying to understand the money requirements."

"Don't you think you ought to figure out what you want to be doing first?" Bill looked at him with eyebrows raised.

"Hmm … that's a great point, Bill. Maybe I'd better give that some more thought, too!"

Bill smiled as he remembered the conversation. It seemed a little reverse to him at the time, to try to decide on the form of the business before deciding on what the business was going to do.

And then there was the conversation he had at the outplacement office with another job seeker named Peter, who was wondering if he might look at jobs in the not-for-profit world.

"I think I could take my business experience and put it to good use in a not-for-profit organization." Peter and Bill were sitting at a table in the office coffee room.

"Have you ever worked at a not-for-profit?" asked Bill. "Or been on the board of one?"

Peter shook his head. "No to both. But they're always looking for good people, and I think I can contribute."

"I've been on a board or two." Bill took a drink of his decaf. "It's true, they're always looking for good people, but there are two issues. One, open positions for paid staff are rare, and two, if there are any, the positions don't pay at the same scale as the corporate world."

"I know that." Peter nodded. "I'm okay with that as long as the salary is manageable. I just don't know a lot of people in the non-profit world."

Bill took the opportunity to offer his feedback. "Maybe you should think about introducing yourself to the directors of all the local non-profits. And also some board members, too."

The men went on to discuss different ways to reach out to those people and introduce Peter's strengths as benefits to the organizations.

Sitting in front of his computer at home, Bill realized that since that conversation with Peter, he hadn't seen him around the office. He wondered how Peter was doing with introducing himself to the non-profit world. Typing rapidly, he sent a short email off to Peter asking about his progress.

By now Bill was feeling more comfortable in his own search, being able to reach out and connect with people who might point him in the direction of opportunities that were similar to what he had done before. He was also at ease with following up on positions that he had applied for, to keep himself in the minds of the hiring folks.

What he was less sure about were the opportunities outside his comfort zone, the possibilities of starting or owning a business, or even working for a non-profit.

Just then, his cell phone rang. Bill looked at the display. It was Rachel.

"Hey, how's my little girl doing?"

"Good, Dad. How are you?"

"Pretty good. What's new?"

"I've had a couple of on-campus interviews. Not that much going on, though, since the companies have cut back on traveling to colleges. At least, that's what the Career Services office says." Rachel was sitting on a bench outside the library.

"Well, it's true. Everyone's cutting back, especially if it has to do with traveling." Bill leaned back in his chair and put his feet up on the desk. "Have you sent out any letters to anything you've seen on the Web?"

"Yes, just like you told me to, Dad. I've tried to reach out as much as I can, if I see an opening that seems to fit my background."

"Any responses?"

"Not yet, but it's only been a couple of weeks." Rachel stood up and started walking to her next class. "How are things going with you?"

"Oh, okay. I've got my applications submitted to where there are jobs like the one I had. I'm just trying to figure out what else I might be interested in."

"Like what?"

Bill took his feet off the desk and stood up to stretch. "Like if I might want to start a business or maybe buy one."

"Dad, you know I don't know that much about business yet, but if someone wants to sell his business, doesn't that mean that it's not doing well?" Rachel crossed the lawn toward where her next class was going to meet.

Bill sat back down again. "Great question, but not necessarily. The owner could have had enough and just want to do something else. Or, the business could be not doing that well, but with a new owner and a fresh start, it could grow. There are a few reasons to sell that aren't necessarily bad."

"Have you looked at any businesses yet?"

"No, but I have some referrals from the outplacement office to business brokers, so I'll have to check them out."

"Well make sure you do, Dad! Gotta run to class now."

They ended their call. That girl can be quite a taskmaster, thought Bill, as he closed his phone.

He looked at the clock. 11:30. Bill was going to meet Carolyn for lunch today. He gathered his things and headed to the garage.

"Any new thoughts on the opportunities that are different from what you were doing before?" Carolyn and Bill were now seated at the bakery café near her office.

"Not really. This morning I was just doing some reading on the Web about different companies. I'm not sure that –"

He looked down at the table as the café pager interrupted with its buzzing. "I'll go get our food. Be right back."

Bill returned with the sandwich baskets, put Carolyn's in front of her and sat back down in his seat.

"Thanks, dear. You're not sure about what?" Carolyn picked up the pickle and bit into it.

Bill took a napkin. "I'm not sure about us doing our own thing right now. Most of the businesses that I'm interested in would take a pretty good investment of cash upfront. And I'm a little nervous about putting out money right now."

As Bill took a large bite out of his sandwich, Carolyn said, "Being your own boss would give you lots of flexibility."

Bill could only nod, his mouth full of food. A minute later he was able to answer.

"It would, but I think I'd be too worried about the cash flow." He wiped his mouth with a napkin. "We'd have to spend money before we could make any."

"But that's the case for any business you might start, right?"

"Right, but at least for now anyway, I'm not sure I've got the stomach for it." Bill looked at his wife. "Why, do you?"

Carolyn shook her head. "No, I don't. But I didn't want that to stand in your way if you thought you did."

Picking up his sandwich again, Bill said, "Nope, it's not for me right now."

"Are you still going to talk to those business brokers you mentioned?

Bill shrugged, chewing thoughtfully. He swallowed. "I don't know. Maybe, if I feel like it."

Carolyn took a drink from her bottle of juice. "So do you think you are going to stay focused on the same type of job that you had?"

"I think so." Bill looked out the window, drumming his fingers on the table top. "I've got my applications in at a few places now, so I'll be following those up over the next couple of weeks."

"At least those are jobs where you could walk right in and get down to work."

Bill shook his head. "No, not really. I think things have changed out there. Remember, I've been with the last company for 15 years. Most of the companies I'm applying to weren't even around when I started."

Carolyn looked across the table at her husband. "Why is that important? You still know your stuff. Younger companies would want your experience."

"I don't think my experience is the issue. I think it's me." He leaned back and stroked his jaw.

Answering the question implied by his wife's puzzled look, he said, "I think I'll need to adjust my perspective." Pushing his chair back, he continued.

"I was thinking about this earlier today. I was at the last company for 15 years. In that time I became very comfortable. Sure, I did different things and got promotions, but I was still part of the organization that I had known for so long."

Bill paused while he took a drink from his soda.

"The culture of the company became part of me, and I became part of the culture. I was a known entity. I was part of the company's history. Well, I'm no longer a part. Anywhere I go next, the culture will be completely new to me."

He leaned forward for emphasis. "And that might be the biggest change for me yet. I realized this morning that I got pretty comfortable working there, and probably took some things for granted. Wherever I end up next, I can't take anything for granted, and I will have to prove myself all over again."

Carolyn held her hand up in protest. "I'd have a hard time believing that you would have to start from scratch again, after all those years of experience running product lines."

"I didn't say I would have to start from scratch. I just said that I might have to prove myself again. In my next opportunity, they won't know me, like I was known in my last one." Bill finished the last of his soda with a big gulp.

"So what does that mean that you have to do? You mentioned some of the other people at the career center signing up for classes. Is that something that you think you need to do?" Carolyn had a quizzical look on her face.

"No, that's not what I meant. I might need to update my knowledge in some areas, but I can do that on my own by surfing the 'Net. I meant that I need to transform myself from thinking that I'm in front of the curve, to realizing that I may be behind it."

He sat back in his chair, silent for a moment, then looked up at Carolyn with a sheepish grin.

"This is harder to admit than I thought, but I got pretty comfortable the last couple of years at the company. I think that's when I started taking things for granted. And when I started taking things for granted, that's probably when I lost my competitive edge."

Bill straightened. "That's also why you noticed that my energy for the company was kind of flat for the last two or three years."

Carolyn nodded slowly, absorbing what her husband was saying. "So, what do you do about it?"

"Two things, I think. The first is to transform and update my knowledge where I need to. There are things going on at some of the companies that I could learn more about. The second thing is to transform my attitude."

His wife gave him that raised eyebrow look again.

Bill grinned. "That really was harder than I thought it would be to admit it. I've just gotten stale the last couple of years. I lost my passion, my competitive fire."

His expression sobered for a moment. "Maybe that's what caused me to be on the list."

Bill's look quickly changed to one of determination. "This whole thing caught me completely by surprise. I never thought I'd ever be laid off, because I'd been there so long."

He unconsciously clenched his fist as his arm lay on the table. "But in the end, this change will be good for me. It will get my competitive juices flowing again."

Bill glanced at his watch and looked at his wife. "You'd better get back."

Carolyn rose and gave her husband a quick hug. "I'm glad you're working through it all."

"Well, making some headway at least." He and his wife left the restaurant. On the sidewalk, he asked her, "You want a lift?"

"No, I'll walk. I could use the exercise after that big sandwich. See you tonight!" With that, Carolyn headed off, and Bill walked to his car and climbed in.

He started the car and thought, what a revelation. I never thought I was a guy with an attitude problem, but it probably was lack of attitude that caused the problem for me.

Won't make that mistake again, he decided. Bill put the car in gear and drove off, headed back home.

Takeaways – "T" is for "Transform"

The next stop in your career is going to fall into one of four categories:

- Same (or similar) job, same/similar industry
- Same job, different industry
- Different job, same industry
- Different job, different industry

Depending on your geographic area and its business climate, each category will have varying levels of opportunity. And depending on the category you are aiming at, you might need to transform yourself by adding new job skills and/or new industry knowledge.

A fifth category could be self-employment. For many people who transition from a company environment to being self-employed, they transfer much of the knowledge and skills they already have into their business. But you have to *really want* to be in business for yourself.

As you consider opportunities, see which category they fall into. How would you need to transform yourself, to put yourself in a position to compete for the job? What are the gaps you need to fill? Would you consider a longer commute, a relocation, a salary change?

Get a feel for your passion for the opportunities you're considering. If things have been a little stale in your last or current position, now is the time to be conscious of what gets your competitive juices flowing again. You'll be a stronger candidate for it. And if you land a position you have real interest in, you're more likely to do well at it.

Chapter 6 – Implement

Bill was back in the outplacement office again. The intervening couple of weeks had gone by quickly. Some interviews, by phone and in-person, had developed, leaving him with some sense of optimism. It helped that he was able to put himself back in the shoes of the hiring managers again, so he could present the best face as a candidate.

When he wasn't in interviews or following up, Bill hadn't spent a lot of time in the career office, since he was more comfortable doing his online research from his home. But he found catching up with some of the other job seekers a good break from the solitude of Web surfing and phone calls.

It was really a matter of personal preference. Some people preferred having an office to go to regularly. Others, like Bill, would stop in less frequently and work more from their homes.

Just as he rounded the corner from the coffee room, Bill almost bumped into Peter, the man who had been considering working for not-for-profit companies.

"Hey Bill! I've been meaning to get back to you." Peter had not replied to Bill's email from a couple of weeks back, asking about his search for a position.

"Good to see you! How's the search going for non-profits?"

Peter's expression drooped at the question. "I haven't really been able to make much progress with it.

There don't seem to be a lot of positions available, and I haven't been making many connections."

"Did you reach out to some board members and other folks connected with those groups?"

Peter scratched his head. "No, I haven't been able to. I've been trying to get introductions, but no luck meeting people who can connect me. Like I told you last time, I don't know that many people in the non-profit world to start with."

Bill was puzzled. "Well, did you go to the organizations directly?"

"Uh, no." Peter seemed bewildered. "I don't know any of the directors. I mean, I know their names and contact information, but I don't know them personally. I was hoping to connect through social media channels or get referred somehow, but haven't been able to do so."

"Why not just send them a letter and resume, then pick up the phone to follow up?" Bill was really perplexed by the other man's apparent inaction.

Peter didn't say anything. He just looked at Bill and shrugged his shoulders.

"I ... I guess I was waiting for the right introduction."

"But you took the time to find out who the organizations are, and who's in charge, right?"

Peter nodded.

"Then dive in, man!" Bill clapped Peter on the shoulder, startling him.

"What do you mean, dive in?"

"I mean, dive in! Dive into action. Work your plan. You wanted to look into the non-profit world, right? Well, call 'em up and see what they have to offer!"

"But I don't know any of the executives…"

"You don't have to," interrupted Bill. "Just contact them and let them get to know you."

Bill's instincts for the game of hiring had returned in the past few weeks, as he became more comfortable with his job of finding a job. What he remembered from his days as a hiring manager were coming back into focus, so he could now apply those instincts from the candidate side of the fence.

"You're probably thinking that if your background is not connected with what these folks expect to see, you probably can't get in."

Peter nodded.

"The truth is, if you can show how your experience can bring them even greater value because, say, you have a fresh outside perspective, then you could get their attention even more than someone from their own industry." In his enthusiasm for the topic, Bill was almost lecturing Peter.

Peter raised his palms upward. "I was assuming that they wouldn't be interested in someone with an unrelated background, unless they were personally referred."

"You can't assume that," said Bill, shaking his head. "Just dive in and get their attention, then see if they're interested."

Peter seemed re-energized. "I'll do that!" he exclaimed. "And I'll let you know how it goes."

He almost ran down the hallway to collect his jacket. Bill chuckled, shook his head, and returned to the computer he had been using. Just then his phone rang. He glanced at the display and smiled.

"So how's my little girl doing?"

"Hi Dad. What's new?"

"Not much. Just finished chatting with Peter here at the office."

"Did I catch you in the middle of something?" In her dorm room, Rachel was holding the phone with her shoulder while changing into her workout clothes.

"No, I'm going to head back home soon, though. I just stopped in here to check on a couple of things." Bill was standing, getting his jacket on. "How is your job search going?"

"I had a couple more interviews on campus in the past few days. I think one of the companies I talked to by phone last week might want to have me interview with them." Rachel almost got the phone tangled up with a sweatshirt she was trying to get over her head.

"That's great!" exclaimed her father. "Where would it be?"

"Down in the city," replied Rachel, lacing up her running shoes. "I'll take the train and just go for the day."

"When do you find out?" By now Bill was out of the office, walking toward the elevator. He decided to take the stairs.

"They said they'd call me back in the next couple of days." Rachel was always the cautiously optimistic type. "So, we'll see."

"Well, good luck, Rache."

"What about you, Dad? Have you heard from any companies?"

Bill filled his daughter in quickly on his progress. While his activity with the companies he applied to was encouraging, he too was cautious. But cautiously optimistic was always a good thing. Certainly better than impulsively pessimistic.

"Is there any one particular company you like better than the others?" Rachel asked.

"They're all pretty interesting," replied her father. "They all have their pros and cons."

"Like what?"

"Well, one job requires a lot of travel. About three weeks out of four." Bill was now on the first floor of the building and walking out the front door to his parked car. He unlocked it and got in.

"I don't think Mom would like it if you traveled that much, would she?" asked Rachel.

"Probably not. I'm not sure I would, either. Another job would require a long commute."

"Like how long?" Rachel finished throwing some things into a gym bag while she spoke.

"45 minutes to an hour, each way. But at least I'd be in town more."

"So which one are you going to take? I mean, if you got them all." Rachel sometimes had that youthful optimism, too.

Bill laughed. "Well, that would be amazing if they all came through, but even I am not counting on it." He stared straight out the windshield in thought before continuing.

"I don't know. I think I'll have to see how it goes. I'm at different points with different companies. With some I've only had first interviews, and with others I'm going in for the second time. I'll have to see."

"Sounds good, Dad. I'm going to go to the gym now. Have you been keeping up?"

"Yep, I have. I've been using the weight machine almost every morning, and jumping on the elliptical on the off days. I've got to burn off some of this nervous energy, now that I have my passion back!"

Bill paused and felt a twinge of emotion. "Say, when are you coming home, Rachel?"

"I've got a break in a couple of weeks. I'll be back home then, unless I have to go interview somewhere." She was already out her dorm building's door and on her way to the gym across campus.

"Okay, talk to you soon, Rache."

"Bye Dad."

Bill flipped his phone closed.

Takeaways – "I" is for "Implement"

You've scoped out your possible opportunities. You've done a lot of thinking about what it is that you have passion for, or are at least interested in. Hopefully you've got some things going, with some irons in the fire warming up.

So Dive into ACTION! What's that you say? You've already done so? Well, great! Keep on diving, and don't let up. Implement your plan of action, the people you still haven't spoken with yet, the opportunities you haven't finished looking into yet, the industries you haven't learned completely about yet.

It's okay to take breaks, to get away from it all and recharge yourself. Take the afternoon off during the week sometime to do something fun. Or take a whole day off when it looks to be quiet. Take a short vacation if you feel you can, but one warning. If you're going to stress out about the cost of getting away, do something less costly.

When you get back from your breaks, dive in again. Keep working your action plan, investigating, following up, discovering, learning more, brushing up. Never fall into the trap of wait-and-see-what-develops. Apparently even Pete Seeger, the American folk singer, had something to say about this: "Do-so is more important than say-so."

Dive into ACTION!

Chapter 7 – (Be) Objective

Another two weeks went by. Bill continued to have some progress with his search, but no closure or offers just yet. During that time he had a couple of second interviews with more senior managers, and had follow-up requests to contact his references. Cautiously optimistic continued to be his watch phrase.

Rachel was home from college for the short break. She had gone to the city for a day to interview with the company that contacted her, but had not heard anything back from them yet. Father and daughter were in the same state of mind, waiting to hear.

It was the middle of the morning, and they were sitting in the family room. Carolyn was at work.

"I wish they'd get back to me and at least let me know what they're thinking," complained Rachel.

"Well, why don't you ask?" said Bill.

"What do you mean, call them up and say, 'Hey have you made up your mind yet?'"

Bill grinned. "Why not?"

"Won't that be too pushy, like showing them that I want the job?"

"Well, you want the job, don't you?"

Rachel thought for a minute. "Well, I suppose so. But if you tell them, won't that make it look like you're desperate?"

Bill laughed. "Maybe you don't want to appear *desperate*, but you definitely want to appear interested. Desperation and interest are two different things."

He put his foot up on the coffee table. "Calling them up and telling them that you're still interested is a way to keep you on their minds, too."

Rachel looked at her father, then suddenly stood up. "Okay, I'll do it." She went upstairs to her room to get her phone.

Just then, Bill's phone rang.

"Hello, Bill McNolten."

"Hi Bill, it's John Stanyan." John was the hiring manager at one of the companies Bill had applied to.

Bill sat up straight. "Hi John, how are you?"

"Pretty good, Bill. Got a minute?"

"Absolutely." Without realizing it, he stood up as John continued.

"Well I've got to tell you that the guys here were impressed with your visit, and with the things you talked about if you were to come work here."

"I appreciate that, John." Bill didn't realize he had been holding his breath. He exhaled.

"I contacted your references, and of course they had good things to say about you." John chuckled. "I would have been worried if they didn't, since you gave me their names.

"But after talking with everyone on the team, and my boss too … we'd like to make you an offer to join us."

Bill had to restrain himself from letting out a whoop.

"I really appreciate that, John," he said in an unbelievably calm voice. "I think you guys have some real opportunities there."

"So give me a couple of days for me to get a package put together, and I'll mail the details to you. Sound good Bill?"

"Sounds great John. Thanks very much."

"Any concerns or issues from your end, Bill?" asked the manager. "You know the amount of travel that's part of the job, right?"

Bill paused. This was the job that required travel three weeks every month. He answered carefully.

"Yes, I do. It's a consideration, obviously, because of the amount. But I promise you I'll give it serious consideration."

"Okay, that's all I ask."

The men concluded their call. Just as Bill pushed the End button on his phone, Rachel came back into the family room.

"Well?" Bill asked his daughter.

"I didn't get to speak to the man I interviewed with, but I left a message and told him I was still interested."

Rachel plopped down on the couch again and looked up at her father, who was still standing.

"Did I hear you talking to someone down here?" she asked.

Bill sat down next to her. "Yep. I got a call from one of the companies I interviewed with. They offered me a job!"

Rachel bolted upright and exclaimed, "Wow Dad, that's great! Are you going to take it?"

Her father's face clouded over. "Actually, I'm not sure. But I'm going to wait until the official offer comes in before I decide."

"Why, what's the matter?"

"This was the job that required a lot of travel," Bill explained. "And you know that I'm not crazy about the prospect of that, at least at this point in my life."

"But this is your first offer, isn't it?" Rachel was a little puzzled by her father's hesitation.

He nodded. "It's the first and only offer, at the moment."

"So you can't turn it down, then, could you?"

"Well Rache, I don't know. I might. I have to take the long view on this." Bill leaned back on the couch and looked at his daughter.

"If I'm on the road all the time, I know your mom wouldn't like it. I wouldn't like it. And that might affect the way I do my job." He looked out the glass door that opened onto their deck, studying the trees beyond.

"Remember, you get paid for performing. If you like what you do, chances are you'll have more energy and passion, and you'll do a better job. If you don't like what you do, or if something about your job bothers you, then chances are you won't have as much energy and you won't perform as well."

He turned from looking out the window and met Rachel's gaze.

"That happened to me in my last job, and may have cost me the job. I don't want to have that happen again."

"So … when do you decide?" she asked.

"After the offer comes in the mail. I'll decide then. Of course, I'll talk it over with your mom first, too."

"Well, I'm going back to school tomorrow, so I guess you won't know by then, huh?"

"Nope, but don't worry, you'll be the first to know once I figure it out."

B ill brought the mail in from the mailbox and put it on the kitchen island. The offer letter took a few days longer to arrive, but the envelope was in the pile he just carried in. He found the letter opener in the drawer and used it to open the envelope.

The offer was what he expected. No mention of the amount of travel, of course, but he knew the requirements of the position.

He thought back to the lengthy discussion he and Carolyn had about this, a couple of nights before.

"When that offer comes in, what will you do with it?" Carolyn asked. She was mixing butter into a bowl of mashed potatoes. Bill stood by the cutting board, carving a roast chicken.

"Not sure. You know how much travel is involved with this job, right?" Bill cut off a drumstick and put it on the serving plate next to the board.

"Something like three out of four weeks, right?" The microwave beeped, signaling that the carrots were ready. She opened the door and took out the dish.

"Right." Bill put the knife down on the board and turned to his wife. "And I don't think I want to be away from you that long."

Carolyn turned to face him. "But that's your only offer right now. Are there any others that might come along soon?"

Bill folded his arms and leaned against the counter. "There's no way to know. I've had some second interviews and reference checks, but they're still deciding. I think one company might still be bringing in candidates." He picked up the knife again and resumed carving.

"Are you okay with the job itself?" Carolyn mixed in a little salt and butter with the carrots.

"The job would be great. The company has some good potential. I just don't think I want to travel that often." He finished his work with the knife and washed his hands under the faucet.

Drying his hands, he continued, "It is a little scary, though. What if I turn this one down, and we don't get another offer for a long time?" He paused and couldn't resist mentioning the unthinkable.

"Or ever?"

Carolyn put the bowls with the potatoes and carrots on the table. She went over to Bill and put her hands on his arms.

"C'mon dear, you can't think in those terms. You've got a few things going on, so you know deep down that something might come out of those, or might lead to something else later on."

Bill gazed at his wife and nodded. "I know. It's just scary, possibly turning down an offer without another one to take." He took the plate of chicken and put it on the table. They both sat down to their dinner.

Bill continued, "Of course, it wouldn't be right to take a job and still be looking at other possibilities."

He took some chicken and put it on his plate. "What do you think I ought to do with this offer?"

"I don't want you to feel like you have to take the job if you don't think it's going to be right for us," replied Carolyn. She was creating a gravy bowl in the center of her mashed potatoes. "We still have my salary coming in, and for the past couple of years we've been pretty conservative with our finances anyhow."

The McNoltens had been careful with their spending, putting money away when they could, while not overspending on other things.

"Sure, for the short term, we're probably okay, especially with my severance package, but I don't want to run it out." Bill took a bite of chicken and chewed thoughtfully. For the next few minutes they ate silently.

Bill put his fork down and looked at his wife. "I think I'm going to turn it down. I hope I'm making the right decision – for us."

Carolyn put her fork down too. "You are. Don't worry about me. You have to think in terms of how it would be for you."

Bill looked down at his plate. "When I try to be objective about this, and take the long view of things, I don't think it's the right thing for us. I'd be away from home too much."

Carolyn nodded and smiled. "And you know how much I like having you in town."

He raised his glass in a toast. "So here's to other offers coming our way!" They clinked their glasses.

Remembering the conversation, Bill finished reading the offer letter and put it on the island countertop. He pulled out his phone and dialed his wife's office number.

"Hello?"

"Hi honey, it's me. I just brought in the mail. The offer letter arrived." Bill pointed at it for emphasis, even though he was alone in the house.

"Was it what you expected?" Carolyn turned to look out the window in her office.

"Yes. Just as we expected. And as we discussed, I'm going to call them and decline it."

"Okay honey. Good luck with the call."

In their kitchen, Bill took a deep breath and exhaled slowly.

"Bill? Are you still there?"

"Yes. I hope I … we … are making the right decision."

"We are, honey. I know we are."

Ending the call with his wife, Bill started to make his next call. To John, the man who sent him the offer letter sitting on the countertop.

He took another deep breath as the phone started to ring on the other end.

Takeaways – "O" is for "Objective"

It may be the second hardest thing to do, behind accepting your situation, and that is to be objective about what your next step will be. When presented with only one option that may not be ideal, and no idea of when the next option will present itself, it's difficult to be impartial.

But you need to try to be objective about it, because if you make a short-term decision that in the long run is not the right one, you may be faced with the same situation all over again. If you take a job that you have no passion for or even any interest in, you could probably make it work for a short while – weeks, months, maybe even a year.

Eventually, it will catch up to you. Going to work will get harder and harder, and it will reflect in the way you perform. And then you might find yourself having to look for another new position, as the cycle repeats.

We all might not have the option to do what Bill did in the chapter when he turned down the first offer. But you must think it through to see both sides of the decision, and look at it from a long-term perspective. Then if you decide to make a decision in the short-term, at least you'll have considered the long-term.

If it doesn't feel right, maybe it's not right. Think with your head, but be sure to listen to your heart, too.

Chapter 8 – Nerves

More days and weeks went by. Bill was beginning to wonder if he should have taken that position with lots of travel after all. When he spoke with the hiring manager, John, to turn down the offer, he was understanding.

"Now, I just want to make sure, Bill … was there any issue with our offer?"

"John, it was a great offer. I appreciate it very much. I just don't think that the high level of travel is going to be the best match for me right now. And I know there's no other way to do that job well."

"Did somebody else outbid us, by chance?" John laughed as if he never expected anyone to outbid them.

"No, not at all," answered Bill. "I am considering other opportunities as we speak, but I just wanted to get back to you so you could do what you need to do to fill your position quickly with the best person."

"I appreciate your honesty very much," admitted John. "There are a lot of people who would have left us hanging while they see what else develops." He laughed again. "Besides, I thought you were the best person for the job!"

The call ended with John graciously telling Bill that if he were to change his mind, check in with him in case they still hadn't filled the job yet.

As Bill reminisced about that conversation, his reverie was interrupted by the gurgling sound of the coffeemaker in the break room coming to the end of its brew cycle. He had chosen to swing by the outplacement office this morning.

Bill poured himself a cup of decaf and reached for a packet of sweetener. It was now almost three weeks since the conversation with John, and in that time none of the other companies had any news for Bill. He hadn't been eliminated at all, there was just no decision yet.

This was making him more nervous than he was before. That's what turning down an offer without another one in hand can do to you, he thought as he stirred his coffee and took a sip.

"Good morning Bill! How are you?"

Bill looked up as Shirley, the director of the service, walked in and helped herself to some coffee.

"Fine, Shirley. How are you doing?"

Shirley sat down at a table, steam curling up from the cup of coffee in front of her. Bill took a nearby chair.

"I'm good, thanks. Any news?"

Bill shook his head. "No, not yet. The companies are still thinking about it. They all said they had some great candidates come through, and that I am a strong candidate as well."

He took a sip from his cup. "I feel like I'm well-positioned to be seriously considered. But honestly, the waiting can be nerve-wracking."

Shirley smiled. "You know the old saying. 'Nerves are good. It means you care.' "

"Well, I don't know if nerves are all that good for me. I haven't been able to sleep much lately."

Both Bill and Shirley looked up as the man who said those words entered the room. It was Howard, a new client of the office. He poured himself a cup of coffee, and took a seat at the table before continuing.

"I know I care, but I'd like to get a little more sleep while I'm caring!" He laughed, a little nervously.

Bill asked, "What do you do to burn off the nervous energy?"

Howard looked at him, confused. "What do you mean?"

"Do you run?" answered Bill. "Do you work out in the gym? Go for walks? You have to get rid of that excess energy, or else you'll drive yourself crazy. I do something every morning, whether it's lifting weights or getting some cardio on my elliptical."

Shirley added, "You want to turn the negative – nervous – energy into a positive flow. Otherwise you spend all your time worrying or being nervous."

"Well, I guess that's how I spend my time, being nervous," concluded Howard. He nodded toward Bill. "To answer your question, I don't really do anything regular. I belong to a gym, and probably should be going more often, but I've been spending my time getting my search off the ground."

Bill drained his coffee cup. "Maybe that's why you're not getting much sleep, Howard. Nerves may be good, but you don't want to get too much of a good thing."

He rose to toss his empty cup into the wastebasket. "And it sounds like you're getting too much of a good thing." Bill pointed at Howard's cup and grinned. "Maybe you should try decaf!"

Howard laughed again, nervously. "Very funny, Bill."

"Bill's got a point," said Shirley. "If you don't get to burn off that nervous energy, you could appear nervous. When you make approaches during your job search, you want to be relaxed and confident, not nervous."

Howard looked at the other two. "I don't seem nervous now, do I?"

Bill glanced over at Shirley. "Uh, I'll let you talk to Shirley about that. I have to head out now. Good luck, Howard!"

He said goodbye to both, and left the office suite to return to his car. As he pulled out of the parking lot, Bill stopped for a moment and looked at the office building in his rearview mirror. Turning onto the road, he accelerated and started to make his way back to his house.

Nerves are good, indeed. If it just wasn't so nerve-wracking at times.

Takeaways – "N" is for "Nerves"

This whole process is a nervous time, but that's okay. Use the nervous energy to your advantage. Turn it into passion and energy for the opportunities you are chasing, and for the things you are trying to accomplish.

Unfocused nervous energy can make you look exactly that, nervous. Focused nervous energy looks very much like passion and a sense of urgency. People like working with energetic people, because they give everyone energy. People don't like working with nervous people, because they make everyone nervous. Smooth out the rough edges of all this energy by taking breaks once in awhile, but more importantly by getting regular exercise.

Go for a run, a bike ride, a brisk walk, a jaunt on the treadmill. Lift some weights until you feel it, or just climb the stairs in your home for ten minutes. Swim laps, tread water, or go hit some tennis balls. Do whatever it is you choose to burn that excess nervous energy, which can put you in a negative light.

Don't spend too much time sweating about things you don't have any control over. Remember that in most cases, you have nothing to lose and everything to gain. Turn that nervous energy into a positive burn that you can focus on your action plan like a booster rocket.

Nerves are good. It means you care. But don't let it make you nervous. That would be too much of a good thing.

Epilogue – Three Months Later

The phone rang, on the desk in the third floor office.

"Hello, Bill McNolten speaking."

"Hi Dad!"

Bill broke into a big grin. "Hey, how's my little girl doing?"

"Okay, Dad." Rachel smiled at her father's familiar opening. "But I'm not so little anymore, you know."

Bill followed the rest of the script. "Well, you know what I say … you'll always be my little girl, even when you're all grown up." He leaned back in his chair and looked out his window, onto the parking lot below. "So, how's it going with your new job?"

"Really good, Dad," replied Rachel. "The work is challenging, the people are nice – it's looking pretty good so far. And I like being in the city, too."

"Well, that's terrific." Bill nodded his head with satisfaction.

"And what about you? How is your job going?"

"Same story as yours, Rache. Good people, interesting work. Good potential here, too. And I'm glad my competitive fire is back again. That was missing the last couple of years at the other place."

"Are you glad you waited for this job to come along, instead of taking the first one that was offered to you?"

Bill smiled at the memory of it all. "Remember, I didn't know that this job would come along, at the time I turned down the other one. So that was a nervous few weeks for me in between."

Miles away, in her cubicle at work, Rachel leaned back in her chair and smiled too. "I remember."

They spent the next few minutes chatting more about their respective positions.

"But didn't you say your job was going to be kind of a step back for you, Dad?"

Bill switched the phone to his other ear. "Not a step back, but I knew there were some things I would be doing that I had done years ago. But that's not really an issue for me. There are also new challenges that I've never had before, so I'm learning new things."

Rachel thought about that for a moment. "I guess you're right, Dad."

"Aren't I always?" Bill grinned into the phone. "So, I'd better get back to work, and you, too. When do I get to see my little girl again?"

"How about a couple of weekends from now?"

"Sounds good. I'll talk to you before then. Okay?"

"Great, Dad. Say hi to Mom. Love you!"

"Love you too. Take care of yourself." Bill hung up the phone, for a moment his hand still resting on it. He smiled and turned back to the computer on his desk.

ACTION! Summary

A is for **Accept**

C is for **Connect**

T is for **Transform**

I is for **Implement**

O is for **Objective**

N is for **Nerves**

Accept your situation, accept the uncertainty. Move on to creating your personal action plan.

Connect with everyone you know. Maybe even some you don't know, yet.

Transform yourself where you need to. Be open to new possibilities.

Implement your action plan. Dive into ACTION!

Be **Objective** before making decisions that affect you over the long-term.

Nerves are good. It means you care – and it gives you energy.

About the Author

Gary Lim, M.A., is the founder of ActionPronto.com, the business through which he offers "action plan coaching" services, keynote speaking, and seminars. He is president of Aurarius LLC, a management consulting firm he first founded in California's "Silicon Valley" then relocated to Upstate New York. He is also a co-founder of HealthcareBusinessOffice LLC. Gary's past business experience included leadership positions at larger firms such as Hewlett Packard, ROLM, XEROX, and Novell, and at small companies and start-ups.

A seasoned and energetic public speaker, Gary is known as "The Actuator" and has spoken to audiences in many venues, including keynote addresses, conference workshops, corporate/executive seminars, product launches, and training courses. He has worked with thousands of attendees from organizations ranging from Fortune 500 corporations and mid-market firms to not-for-profits and educational institutions. His coaching client base continues to grow.

As an author, *Dive Into ACTION!* is Gary's third released book. His first, *The Road to Gumption: Using Your Inner Courage to Balance Your Work and Personal Life* (Dorato Press) was an Amazon #1 Bestseller in its category. Next came *Let It Fly! Defy the Laws of Business Gravity and Keep Your Company Soaring* (Dorato), a business parable featuring effective business leadership principles and a story set at a well-known golf course along the Pacific Ocean. Gary's fourth book, *Get CRAZY About What You Do! Take Your Success to New Heights* will be completed soon.

In his work with coaching clients, seminar attendees, and company meetings, Gary is often considered among the best at assessing a complex business or personal situation, identifying the critical issues, and offering practical insight for solutions.

He earned a Bachelor's degree *cum laude* from Princeton University, and a Master's degree in organizational management from University of Phoenix.

For more information on action plan coaching services, turn the page. To book speaking engagements and seminars, you can find more details on the Web, or contact Gary directly:

Coaching Web site: www.ActionPronto.com
Book information: www.BooksByGaryLim.com
Email contact: info@ActionPronto.com
Phone contact: 315-885-1532 (direct to Gary)

He can speak more about addressing customized needs, such as:

- Keynote speeches

- Breakout sessions

- Seminars

- Volume pricing for coaching services

- Volume pricing on books

ACTION PLAN COACHING
SERVICES

There are several levels of "action plan coaching" services that Gary Lim offers, including the Inner Circle, Diamond Level, and Emerald Level. The levels are differentiated by subject matter, response time, and method of communication.

The highest level, the Inner Circle, is for existing or budding entrepreneurs and company owners/leaders. This is a group of people who wish to get feedback not only on their personal action plans, but also on issues related to company business. The highest level of coaching, one-on-one dialogue with Gary occurs by phone and by email, with the quickest response time. Clients in the Inner Circle not only have a personal sounding board at their disposal, but also the ear of an experienced business advisor.

The next level, Diamond Level, is for those who would like timely feedback on their personal action plans: what they need to do to stay on track to find their next great opportunity, what they should be thinking about, what they should be acting on. This interactive dialogue occurs one-on-one with Gary by phone or by email.

The Emerald Level is for those clients whose personal action plans might not require as fast a response time, but who will still benefit from the valuable one-on-one dialogue with Gary. This interaction takes place only through email.

At any time, clients can upgrade from one coaching service level to another. Each level offers unlimited contact with Gary, within the context of the services defined. For more information, visit the ActionPronto Web site and click on Services, or contact Gary:

Phone:	315-885-1532 (direct to Gary)
Web:	www.ActionPronto.com
Email:	info@ActionPronto.com

Notes